The Book of
STEAK

The Book of
STEAK

Cooking for carnivores

LOVE FOOD™

This edition published by Parragon in 2016
LOVE FOOD is an imprint of Parragon Books Ltd

Parragon
Chartist House
15–17 Trim Street
Bath, BA1 1HA, UK

www.parragon.com/lovefood

ISBN: 978-1-4723-0769-9

Printed in China

New photography by Mike Cooper
New recipes and food styling by Lincoln Jefferson
Introduction by Anne Sheasby
Project managed by Alice Blackledge
Designed by Beth Kalynka

Notes for the Reader
This book uses both metric and imperial measurements. Follow the same units of measurement throughout;
do not mix metric and imperial. All spoon measurements are level: teaspoons are assumed to be 5 ml, and
tablespoons are assumed to be 15 ml. Unless otherwise stated, milk is assumed to be full fat, eggs and
individual vegetables are medium, and pepper is freshly ground black pepper. Unless otherwise stated, all
root vegetables should be washed and peeled prior to using.

For best results, use a food thermometer when cooking meat – check the latest government guidelines for
current advice.

Garnishes, decorations and serving suggestions are all optional and not necessarily included in the recipe
ingredients or method.

The times given are an approximate guide only. Preparation times differ according to the techniques used
by different people and the cooking times may also vary from those given. Optional ingredients, variations or
serving suggestions have not been included in the time calculations.

Recipes using raw or very lightly cooked eggs should be avoided by infants, the elderly, pregnant women,
convalescents and anyone suffering from an illness. Pregnant and breastfeeding women are advised to avoid
eating peanuts and peanut products. Sufferers from nut allergies should be aware that some of the ready-
made ingredients used in the recipes in this book may contain nuts. Always check the packaging before use.

WHAT'S YOUR BEEF?

A great tasting steak is as much about the cow it comes from, as the way you cook it. Beef can vary a great deal and the taste and quality of the meat that you buy is dependant on several factors including the breed, age, diet, lifestyle and slaughter of the animal, as well as how long it has been hung before it is butchered or prepared for sale. It might seem like a lot of information to take in, but generally speaking the most important thing to remember is that cattle, and indeed all animals reared for meat, that have been raised humanely and that have been allowed to grow and develop naturally and lead contented, healthy lives, are much more likely to produce meat with a better flavour and texture, than those that have been intensively reared. Now that attitudes to farming are changing, meat that has led a happy life is becoming increasingly easy to come by – you should find a wide range of grades of steak at your local supermarket, and a local butcher will certainly be able to assist you in finding locally reared meat. If you are buying from the supermarket (and let's face it, that's what most of us do) then there are a couple of key elements that you should be aware of when making an informed choice for dinner.

In order to make a truly informed choice about your dinner, you should be aware of a number of factors when buying a good steak – you'll never prepare a truly great steak without first having good meat to cook with

HAPPY COWS

FREE RANGE

Beef sold as 'organic' must comply with strict rules and regulations set by various organizations. Organic beef is produced using environmental and animal-friendly farming methods, taking into account the health and welfare of the animals. As a general rule, organic beef comes from animals that are not intensively reared and are bred without the intervention of synthetic chemical medicines (such as antibiotics and growth-promoting hormones). They graze on certified organic pasture (the use of pesticides on this land is avoided wherever possible) and are fed organic, non-GM (genetically modified) feed. They should also have unrestricted outdoor access for much of the year and if they are not housed inside during the winter, they must have shelter, food and water provided.

Free-range beef is a little less prescriptive, and more broadly means that the animals have been allowed to roam and graze freely outdoors. In terms of beef specifications to be aware of there are also several special breeds and rare breeds, which have distinctive flavours or qualities. Organic, free-range and beef from special breeds will usually be more expensive, but it's well worth buying the best quality beef that you can afford, as it will make for a superior meal.

Of course, all types of beef should look and smell fresh and the meat should be well cut and neatly trimmed. The flesh should be firm to the touch and should look moist but not wet or slimy, and it should be pink or red in colour depending on the type – more mature beef will be darker in colour. The fat should be pale, slightly creamy and firm. Don't shy away from steak that contains flecks of fat throughout – despite the popular conception that all fat is bad, this marbling is considered to make the steak more flavourful and tender. You can't get away from the old adage that 'fat equals flavour'!

If you're buying your meat from the supermarket, then it should include informative labelling as standard, but if you buy beef from a butcher, you will need to ask how the meat has been reared, etc. to gain key information before you purchase it. Butchers are likely to stock a wider range of beef cuts than supermarkets, though many of the big supermarkets now have their own in-store butchers who will be able to offer the same service. Butchers should be able to give specific advice on preparing and cooking the different cuts of beef, where and what breed the meat is from, how long it has been aged or hung, and so on. They can also prepare the beef cuts exactly as you want them – don't be afraid to ask for your steak to be trimmed, or to have a joint tied, it's precisely what you are paying for, so make the most of their expertise. Other suppliers of beef include local farmers' markets, farm shops and mail-order companies specializing in beef and other meats. Always check the 'use-by' date on pre-packaged beef and do not use it after this date.

When specifically buying steaks, look for well-marbled beef that's ideally been aged on the bone for at least two weeks, as this will be more tender and will have much more flavour. Always bring the steak to room temperature before you cook it (this will usually take 30–40 minutes unless specified in the recipe) and oil and season as instructed. Once cooked, steaks need to rest before serving – this allows the fibres within the steak to cool down and stop contracting, resulting in a juicy, tender steak. Loosely 'tent' cooked steak with foil and place in a warm place for the time shown in the recipe.

STORING STEAK

Beef should be stored in a covered container, or wrapped and placed on a dish (so that any juices don't drip and contaminate other foods) in the bottom of the refrigerator for up to 3–5 days (depending on how fresh it is when you buy it), or check the 'use-by' date, if it's provided on the packaging. Minced beef and offal do not keep as well and should be eaten within 1–2 days. If the beef is wrapped in plastic wrapping it is best to remove this (to prevent the meat from sweating) and place the meat in a dish, then cover it before refrigerating.

Beef can also be frozen on the day of purchase and kept for up to 3–6 months. It should then be defrosted in a dish (to catch any juices) in the fridge until completely thawed. Do not refreeze raw beef that has been defrosted; however, if you then use the defrosted beef to make a dish that is then cooked, you can freeze the dish.

IN THE FRIDGE
3–5 DAYS

IN THE FREEZER
3–6 MONTHS

Fore Rib

Also known as best rib and one of the most expensive cuts of beef. Sold as a joint on the bone or as a boneless rolled joint. Ideal for roasting; also suitable for braising. Single rib cutlets are also available and are suitable for grilling, frying and barbecuing.

Prime rib is cut from below the fore rib. One of the most expensive cuts and one of the largest roasting joints. Should be chined to make carving easier. Also sold boned and sliced as rib-eye steaks for frying, grilling and barbecuing.

Chuck & Blade

Often sold as braising, chuck or blade steak. Sold ready-cubed or as slices. Requires long, slow, moist cooking, so is therefore suitable for braising, stewing and casseroling, or for use in pies. Blade steaks may also be available and are suitable for marinating and grilling or frying.

Neck & Clod

Neck is usually sold as stewing steak or mince and is one of the most inexpensive cuts of beef. Clod is a similar cut. Requires long, slow, moist cooking, so is therefore suitable for braising, stewing and casseroling.

Thick Rib

Also known as top rib. Usually sold as a boneless, rolled joint or as steaks for pot-roasting or braising.

Brisket

Sold as a joint on the bone or as a boneless rolled joint and is an inexpensive cut. Sometimes sold salted for boiling. Tends to be quite fatty. Requires long, slow, moist cooking so is suitable for pot-roasting, braising, stewing and boiling (if salted).

Shin

Sold with or without the bone. Requires long, slow, moist cooking so is suitable for stewing, casseroling or braising. It is often used to make brawn.

Thin Rib

This is usually sold boned and rolled or as short ribs (with bones left in). Suitable for casseroling, stewing, braising or pot-roasting.

Silverside

Very lean, boneless joint traditionally sold salted or cured for boiling as salt beef, but also sold unsalted for roasting and barded with fat. Suitable for roasting, braising, pot-roasting or boiling (if salted/cured).

Rump

Lean and tender cut of beef with a narrow edge of fat (not as tender as sirloin and much less tender than fillet). Suitable for grilling, griddling, frying, barbecuing, stir-frying and kebabs, and braising in casseroles (if sold as a single piece).

Topside

Suitable for roasting, braising, casseroling, pot-roasting or stir-frying. Also good cubed and used in pies or for kebabs. Thinly sliced topside steaks (ideal for beef olives) are also available.

Thick flank

Also known as top rump and sometimes sold as braising steak. Suitable for pot-roasting, braising, casseroling and stewing

Leg

Can be sold as braising steak or stewing steak. Sold ready-cubed or as slices. Requires long, slow, moist cooking, so is therefore suitable for braising, stewing and casseroling.

Sirloin

Prime, tender and juicy roasting joint marbled with fat, either sold on the bone or as a boneless rolled joint. Several popular steaks are cut from the sirloin including entrecôte, sirloin, T-bone, fillet, porterhouse and minute. Joints suitable for roasting; steaks suitable for grilling, griddling, frying, barbecuing and stir-frying.

Fillet steak or tenderloin is a very lean cut – and the most tender of all cuts of beef. Steaks suitable for grilling, griddling, frying, barbecuing, stir-frying; whole fillet suitable for roasting or wrapping in pastry and baking (beef Wellington). Also used raw to make carpaccio (thin slices) or steak tartare (finely chopped).

Flank

This cut can be fatty. Often made into mince rather than sold as a piece. Suitable for stewing and braising, or it can be thinly sliced, marinated and stir-fried.

Skirt, like Flank, is also cut from the belly. It usually requires long, slow, moist cooking so is suitable for stewing, braising and pot-roasting, but it can also be marinated and then stir-fried.

Roasting

Best used for cooking tender roasts of meat like fore rib of beef – the roast is seasoned and placed in a hot oven, and cooked, basting as often a possible with the fat that renders out of it, until the meat is done to your liking. Roast beef can be served pink in the middle. Try a tasty crust for extra flavour and texture – like the Ranch Steak with a blue cheese crust on page 24.

Slow-roast

A great way of cooking not-so-tender cuts, that are too tough to roast normally. It's the same as roasting, except the oven temperature is lower, and the meat is given more time to break its fibres down.

Frying

Tender cuts like steaks are often fried in oil or butter in a heavy, hot pan, turning every now and again until they are cooked to your liking. Pair a good steak with a classic sauce, like Béarnaise (page 54) or peppercorn (page 58) and a side of Triple-cooked Chips (page 110).

Grilling

A good alternative to frying steak – make sure that the grill is as hot as possible before putting the meat under. Initially, sear under the high heat, then reduce the temperature to cook through to your liking (giving a crispy outside and juicy inside).

Poaching

A delicate way of cooking tender cuts of meat. Just like fish, meat can be poached in stock and wine, removed when just cooked and served with dressings or sauces to help lift its flavour.

Stewing

Best for cooking tough cuts like shoulder, shin and brisket of beef. The meat is cooked gently and slowly in a pot, either on the hob or in the oven, with vegetables, flavourings (herbs and spices) and either stock, wine, beer or water, until it's tender enough to eat. Stewed in a sticky barbecue marinade, the Thin Ribs on page 38 are the perfect example of when slower is better.

COOKING TIMES

Blue Prepare the steak as instructed, then place in the pre-heated pan and sear both sides of the meat (for about 1 minute each). The steak should be browned on the outside, but still raw in the middle. Set aside and rest as instructed.

Rare Prepare the steak as instructed, then place in the pre-heated pan and sear both sides of the meat (for about 2 minutes each). The steak should be warm through the middle, browned on the outside, but still pink in the centre. Set aside and rest as instructed.

*Cooking times will vary depending on the type and thickness of the steak, and how hot your pan is.

Medium Prepare the steak as instructed, then place in the pre-heated pan and sear both sides of the meat (for about 4 minutes each). The steak should be more brown than pink, but still slightly pink band in the centre. Set aside and rest as instructed.

Medium rare Prepare the steak as instructed, then place in the pre-heated pan and sear both sides of the meat (for about 3 minutes each). The steak should be browned on the outside, but still slightly pink in the centre. Set aside and rest as instructed.

Well done Prepare the steak as instructed, then place in the pre-heated pan and sear both sides of the meat (for about 5 minutes each). The steak should be brown all the way through. Set aside and rest as instructed.

RIB EYE STEAK IN A BOOZY BOURBON MARINADE

Blade Steak in a green herb marinade

22 DRUNK CHUCK STEAK I A
RICH RED WINE MARI ADE

RANCH STEAK WITH A BLUE CHEESE CRUST

Beef Short Ribs with bacon and herb sauce

28 SLOW COOKED BRISK T
WITH A SPICY DRY R B

RIB OF BEEF WITH A FIER
HORSERADISH CRUST

34 Butlers' Steak with lemon and basil pesto

SKIRT STEAK WITH BLOODY MARY BUTT R

THIN RIBS IN A STICKY BARBECUE MARINADE

FORTY RIB-EYE STEAK
WITH ROASTED
PEPPER SALSA

PRIME RIB WITH TRADITIONAL HORSERADISH SAUCE

UP FRONT CUTS

Rib-Eye Steak

in a boozy bourbon marinade

Ingredients

FEEDS 4 **PREP 10 mins** **COOK 10 mins**

4 rib-eye steaks,
350 g/12 oz each
2 tbsp olive oil
2 tbsp butter

marinade
2 tbsp extra virgin
olive oil
200 ml/7 fl oz good
quality bourbon
1 small bunch thyme,
leaves picked
1 tsp dried oregano
2 garlic cloves, crushed
1 tsp salt
1 tsp pepper

1. Place all of the marinade ingredients into a shallow non-metallic dish, large enough to hold all of the steaks in a single layer. Mix the ingredients together.

2. Add the steaks to the marinade, turning a few times to coat. Cover and chill in the refrigerator for a minimum of 4 hours, or for up to 12 hours if time allows. Turn once, mid-way through marinating.

3. Remove from the refrigerator 1 hour before cooking, to allow the meat to return to room temperature. Reserve the remaining marinade.

4. Preheat a large frying pan over a high heat and add the oil and butter. Cook the steaks for 5 minutes on each side for medium-rare, or until cooked to your liking. Cook the steaks in batches if necessary. Set aside to rest for 5 minutes before serving.

5. Meanwhile, reduce the heat to medium-high, pour the reserved marinade into the pan, and flambé to create a sauce. Serve the steaks with the sauce poured over the top.

Blade Steak

in a green herb marinade

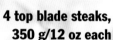
Ingredients

FEEDS 4

PREP 10 mins

COOK 10 mins

4 top blade steaks,
350 g/12 oz each

marinade
4 tbsp olive oil
1 tbsp light muscovado
sugar
2 tbsp red wine vinegar
2 tbsp chopped flat-leaf
parsley
2 tbsp chopped basil
2 tbsp chopped tarragon
2 tbsp chopped thyme
2 garlic cloves, crushed
1 tsp salt
1 tsp pepper

1. Place all of the marinade ingredients into a shallow non-metallic dish, large enough to hold all of the steaks in a single layer. Mix the ingredients together.

2. Add the steaks to the marinade, turning a few times to coat. Cover and chill in the refrigerator for a minimum of 4 hours, or for up to 12 hours if time allows. Turn once, mid-way through marinating.

3. Remove from the refrigerator 1 hour before cooking, to allow the meat to return to room temperature. Discard the marinade.

4. Preheat a griddle pan over a high heat and cook the steaks for 5 minutes on each side for medium-rare, or until cooked to your liking. Cook the steaks in batches if necessary. Set aside to rest for 5 minutes before serving.

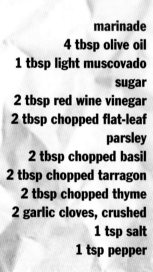

Acidic vinegar in the marinade helps to tenderize the steak, while the herbs give the meat a fresh, light flavour.

Drunk Chuck Steak

in a rich red wine marinade

Ingredients

FEEDS 4 **PREP 10 mins** **COOK 10 mins**

4 chuck steaks,
350 g/12 oz each

marinade
4 tbsp olive oil
100 ml/3½ fl oz good
quality red wine
1 small bunch thyme,
leaves picked
1 small bunch rosemary,
leaves picked
2 garlic cloves, crushed
1 tbsp Dijon mustard
1 tsp salt
1 tsp pepper

1. Place all of the marinade ingredients into a shallow non-metallic dish, large enough to hold all of the steaks in a single layer. Mix the ingredients together.

2. Add the steaks to the marinade, turning a few times to coat. Cover and chill in the refrigerator for a minimum of 4 hours, or for up to 12 hours if time allows. Turn once, mid-way through marinating.

3. Remove from the refrigerator 1 hour before cooking, to allow the meat to return to room temperature. Discard the marinade.

4. Preheat a griddle pan over a high heat and cook the steaks for 5 minutes on each side for medium-rare, or until cooked to your liking. Cook the steaks in batches if necessary. Set aside to rest for 5 minutes before serving.

Ranch Steak

with a blue cheese crust

Ingredients

FEEDS 4

PREP 10 mins

COOK 15 mins

4 ranch steaks,
350 g/12 oz each
1 tsp salt
1 tsp pepper
4 tbsp olive oil

blue cheese crust
2 tbsp olive oil
150 g/5½ oz fresh
breadcrumbs
2 tbsp chopped flat-leaf
parsley
2 garlic cloves, crushed
250 g/9 oz Gorgonzola
cheese, crumbled

1. Preheat the oven to 200°C/400°F/Gas Mark 6. Season the steaks with the salt and pepper, and rub with the olive oil.

2. Preheat a large frying pan over a high heat and seal the steaks on both sides. Transfer the steaks to a large, shallow roasting tray.

3. To make the blue cheese crust, mix together the olive oil, breadcrumbs, parsley and garlic. Crumble the blue cheese over the steaks, then top with the breadcrumb mixture.

4. Place the steaks in the preheated oven and cook for 10–12 minutes or until the cheese has melted and the breadcrumbs have turned golden brown for medium-rare, or cover with foil and return to the oven until cooked to your liking. Remove from the oven and set aside to rest for 5 minutes before serving.

Beef Short Ribs

with bacon and herb sauce

Ingredients

4 bacon rashers, cut into
1-cm/½-inch pieces
1.6 kg/3 lb 8 oz beef
short ribs
1 large onion, diced
1 celery stick, diced
4 garlic cloves,
finely chopped
2 tbsp plain flour
225 ml/8 fl oz dry sherry
750 ml/1¼ pints
beef stock
2 tsp tomato purée
6 fresh thyme sprigs
1 bay leaf
salt and pepper

FEEDS
4

PREP
10 mins

COOK
2½ hours

1. Preheat the oven to 180°C/350°F/Gas Mark 4.

2. Put the bacon in a large casserole and fry over a medium heat until the fat is rendered. Remove the bacon with a slotted spoon and set aside, leaving the fat in the casserole.

3. Increase the heat to medium-high, add the short ribs to the casserole and sear on all sides. Remove from the casserole and set aside. Add the onion and celery, reduce the heat to medium and cook for 5 minutes, or until the onion is soft.

4. Add the garlic and flour to the casserole and cook, stirring, for 2 minutes. Whisk in the sherry, increase the heat to high and bring to the boil. Use a wooden spoon to scrape the sediment from the base of the casserole. Add the stock, tomato purée, thyme and bay leaf, and season generously with salt and pepper to taste.

5. Add the ribs and reserved bacon, cook until simmering, then cover tightly and place in the preheated oven. Cook for 2 hours, or until the meat is tender. Skim any excess fat from the top of the cooking liquid and adjust the seasoning if necessary. Serve with the sauce spooned over the short ribs.

These short ribs are cut 'English style' (parallel to the bone) but you can also buy fattier 'flanken style' (cut across the bone) and cook in the same way.

Slow Cooked Brisket

with a spicy dry rub

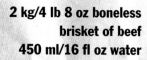

Ingredients

2 kg/4 lb 8 oz boneless
brisket of beef
450 ml/16 fl oz water

spicy dry rub
1 tbsp dried oregano
1 tbsp hot smoked
paprika
1 tbsp cumin seeds
1 tsp garlic salt
1 tsp ground cinnamon
2 tbsp light muscovado
sugar
1 tsp salt
1 tsp pepper

1. Preheat the oven to 160°C/325°F/Gas Mark 3.

2. Place all of the dry rub ingredients in a pestle and mortar and crush to a coarse powder. Alternatively, process in a food processor or blender to achieve the desired consistency.

3. Place the brisket on a large chopping board and sprinkle over the rub mix, turning the brisket to coat. Transfer the brisket to a wire rack over a roasting tray, place in the preheated oven and cook for 1 hour.

4. Remove from the oven and add the water to the roasting tray. Cover the tray with foil and return to the oven for a further 2½ hours.

5. Remove from the oven and test the meat – it should be cooked through and tender. If necessary, return the tray to the oven for a further 30 minutes. Set aside to rest for 10 minutes before serving.

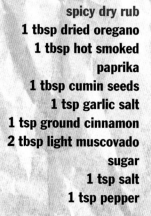

Position the brisket fat-side up in the roasting tray – as the beef cooks and the fat melts, it will baste the meat.

Rib of Beef

with a fiery horseradish crust

Ingredients

FEEDS 4–6 PREP 10 mins COOK 50 mins

2 kg/4 lb 8 oz rib of beef,
on the bone
1 tsp salt
1 tsp pepper
4 tbsp olive oil

horseradish crust
2 tbsp extra virgin
olive oil
4 tbsp creamed
horseradish
2 tbsp English mustard
juice and zest of 1 lemon
½ tsp salt
½ tsp pepper

1. Preheat the oven to 180°C/350°F/Gas Mark 4.

2. Place the beef rib on a large chopping board and season with the salt and pepper.

3. Place all of the horseradish crust ingredients into a small bowl and mix until combined to a rough paste.

4. Heat the olive oil in a large frying pan over a medium-high heat and seal the rib on all sides. Transfer to a wire rack positioned over a roasting tray and brush all over with the horseradish paste. Place the tray in the preheated oven and cook for 50 minutes.

5. Remove the rib from the oven and set aside to rest for 30 minutes before serving. Serve with the juices from the roasting tray poured over.

Butlers' Steak

with lemon and basil pesto

Ingredients

FEEDS 4 **PREP 10 mins** **COOK 10 mins**

4 butlers' steaks,
350 g/12 oz each
2 tbsp olive oil
1 tsp salt
1 tsp pepper

lemon and basil pesto
2 garlic cloves, crushed
zest of 2 lemons
100 g/3½ oz pine nuts
100 g/3½ oz freshly
grated Parmesan cheese
4 tbsp extra virgin
olive oil
1 large bunch basil
½ tsp salt
1 tsp pepper

1. Place the steaks on a large chopping board, rub with the olive oil and season with the salt and pepper.

2. Preheat a griddle pan over a high heat and cook the steaks for 5 minutes on each side for medium-rare, or until cooked to your liking. Cook the steaks in batches if necessary. Set aside to rest for 5 minutes before serving.

3. Meanwhile, place all of the pesto ingredients in a pestle and mortar and crush to a rough paste. Alternatively, process in a food processor or blender, to achieve the desired consistency. Serve the steaks with the lemon and basil pesto.

Skirt Steak

with Bloody Mary butter

Ingredients

FEEDS 4   PREP 10 mins   COOK 10 mins

4 skirt steaks,
350 g/12 oz each
2 tbsp olive oil
1 tsp salt
1 tsp pepper

Bloody Mary butter
150 g/5½ oz unsalted
butter
1 tsp hot sauce
1 tbsp Worcestershire
sauce
1 tbsp horseradish sauce
1 large tomato, peeled,
deseeded and diced
1 tsp celery salt
1 tsp pepper

1. Place the steaks on a large chopping board, rub with the olive oil and season with the salt and pepper.

2. Preheat a griddle pan over a high heat and cook the steaks for 5 minutes on each side for medium-rare, or until cooked to your liking. Cook the steaks in batches if necessary. Set aside to rest for 5 minutes before serving.

3. Meanwhile, mix all of the Bloody Mary butter ingredients together, then spoon on top of the warm steaks before serving.

Thin Ribs

in a sticky barbecue marinade

FEEDS 4 | PREP 10 mins | COOK 3 hours

Ingredients

2 kg/4 lb 8 oz beef short ribs

marinade
1 onion, finely chopped
2 garlic cloves, crushed
2 tbsp English mustard
1 tbsp smoked paprika
1 tbsp dried oregano
1 tbsp smoked chipotle sauce
1 tsp fennel seeds
100 ml/3½ fl oz light soy sauce
100 g/3½ oz dark muscovado sugar
100 ml/3½ fl oz tomato ketchup
100 ml/3½ fl oz cider vinegar
200 ml/7 fl oz water
1 tsp celery salt
1 tsp pepper

1. Place all of the marinade ingredients into a large non-metallic bowl and mix together.

2. Add the ribs to the marinade, cover and chill in the refrigerator for a minimum of 4 hours, or for up to 12 hours if time allows. Turn every couple of hours to coat.

3. Preheat the oven to 180°C/350°F/Gas Mark 4. Place all of the ribs, with the marinade, into a large flameproof casserole with a tight fitting lid. Cover and place in the preheated oven for 3 hours.

4. Remove the dish from the oven and leave to cool slightly, then remove the ribs from the sauce and set aside to keep warm. Skim off any excess fat from the surface of the remaining marinade, then place the casserole dish over a medium heat and reduce to a sticky consistency. Serve with the reduced barbecue marinade drizzled over the ribs.

Rib-Eye Steak

with roasted pepper salsa

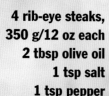 Ingredients

 FEEDS 4

 PREP 10 mins

 COOK 40 mins

4 rib-eye steaks,
350 g/12 oz each
2 tbsp olive oil
1 tsp salt
1 tsp pepper

roasted pepper salsa
1 large red onion,
quartered
4 garlic cloves
2 red peppers, halved
and deseeded
2 yellow peppers, halved
and deseeded
2 tomatoes, halved
2 large red chillies,
medium heat
1 tbsp sweet smoked
paprika
4 tbsp olive oil
1 tbsp dried oregano
2 tbsp sherry vinegar
1 tsp salt
1 tsp pepper
2 tbsp chopped
flat-leaf parsley

1. Preheat the oven to 200°C/400°F/Gas Mark 6.

2. Place all of the salsa ingredients, apart from the parsley, into a large non-metallic mixing bowl. Mix the ingredients together, then transfer to a large shallow roasting tray. Place the tray in the preheated oven for 30 minutes, or until everything is softened and the edges of the vegetables are beginning to blacken. Once cooked, remove the roasting tray from the oven and leave to cool.

3. Meanwhile, place the steaks on a large chopping board, rub with the olive oil, and season with the salt and pepper.

4. Preheat a griddle pan over a high heat and cook the steaks for 5 minutes on each side for medium-rare, or until cooked to your liking. Cook the steaks in batches if necessary. Set aside to rest for 5 minutes before serving.

5. Place all of the roasted salsa ingredients on a chopping board with the parsley, and roughly chop. Serve the salsa alongside the steaks.

For a slightly sweeter salsa, swap the yellow peppers for two handfuls of ripe cherry tomatoes, and roast as instructed.

Prime Rib

with traditional horseradish sauce

Ingredients

FEEDS 2 per rib   **PREP** 5 mins   **COOK** 2–2½ hours

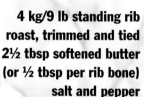

4 kg/9 lb standing rib
roast, trimmed and tied
2½ tbsp softened butter
(or ½ tbsp per rib bone)
salt and pepper

horseradish sauce
6 tbsp creamed
horseradish
6 tbsp soured cream

1. To make the sauce, mix the horseradish and soured cream together in a small bowl. Cover with clingfilm and chill until required.

2. Place the beef in a large roasting tin. Rub the entire surface of the meat with butter and season generously with salt and pepper. Leave to stand at room temperature for 2 hours.

3. Meanwhile, preheat the oven to 230°C/450°F/Gas Mark 8. Put the meat in the preheated oven and roast for 20 minutes to seal the outside. Then reduce the oven temperature to 160°C/325°F/Gas Mark 3 and roast for 2 hours, until the temperature of the meat reaches 43–46°C/110–115°F when tested with a meat thermometer, for medium-rare, or until cooked to your liking.

4. Set aside to rest for 30 minutes before serving. While resting the meat will continue to cook – for medium-rare the final internal temperature will be approximately 54–57°C/130–135°F. Slice and serve with the horseradish sauce.

Top Round Steak with beef gravy

NEW YORK STRIP STEAK WITH TARRAGON MUSHROOMS

FIFTY SIRLOIN STEAK WITH WATERCRESS BUTTER

UMP STEAK SANDWICHES WITH MUSTARD DRESSING

Strip Steak with Béarnaise sauce

PORTERHOUSE STEAK WITH CHILLI AND GARLIC RUB

28 T-BONE STEAK WITH PEPPERCORN SAUCE

STEAKHOUSE BURGERS WITH GRUYERE CHEESE

LANK STEAK IN 'THE BEST' BARBECUE MARINADE

66 Steak Medallions with beef and beer sauce

BEEF WELLINGTON

70 RUMP STEAK WITH A SPICY CHILLI CRUST

RUMP AND REAR CUTS

Top Round Steak

with beef gravy

FEEDS 4–6   PREP 10 mins   COOK 45–50 mins

Ingredients

900-g/2-lb top round steak, 5 cm/2 inches thick
2 tbsp vegetable oil
salt and pepper

marinade
4 tbsp balsamic vinegar
2 tbsp olive oil
4 garlic cloves, crushed
½ tsp dried rosemary

beef gravy
115 g/4 oz butter
½ onion, diced
70 g/2½ oz plain flour
1 garlic clove, finely chopped
1.2 litres/2 pints beef stock
2 tsp tomato purée
1 tsp Dijon mustard
1 tsp Worcestershire sauce

1. To make the marinade, put all of the ingredients into a small non-metallic bowl and whisk together. Put the steak on a plate and prick all over with a fork on both sides. Transfer to a resealable polythene bag and pour in the marinade. Squeeze out the air, seal, and chill in the refrigerator for 12 hours.

2. To make the gravy, melt the butter in a saucepan over a medium heat. Add the onion and cook until softened. Add the flour and cook, stirring, for about 5 minutes, or until the mixture is golden brown. Add the garlic and cook for 30 seconds. Gradually whisk in the stock, then add the remaining ingredients, with salt and pepper to taste. Bring to simmering point, then reduce the heat to low and simmer for 25 minutes, stirring occasionally. Strain into a serving jug and keep warm until ready to serve.

3. Preheat the grill to high. Transfer the steak to a large plate and pat dry. Rub all over with the vegetable oil and season on both sides with salt and pepper. Discard the marinade.

4. Place the steak in a shallow roasting tin and place under the preheated grill. Grill for 7–8 minutes on each side for medium-rare, or until cooked to your liking.

5. Set aside to rest for 10 minutes before serving. Cut into thin slices against the grain and serve.

For extra depth of flavour, add a glass of Madeira wine along with the beef stock when making the gravy.

New York Strip Steak

with tarragon mushrooms

Ingredients

FEEDS 4

PREP 10 mins

COOK 30–35 mins

4 sirloin steaks,
280 g/10 oz each
1 tsp salt
1 tsp pepper
1 tbsp vegetable oil
4 tbsp chicken stock
1 tbsp butter, chilled

tarragon mushrooms
4 tbsp olive oil
2 tbsp butter
900 g/2 lb large button
mushrooms, thickly sliced
2 garlic cloves,
finely chopped
3 tbsp sherry vinegar
1 tbsp chopped fresh
tarragon
salt and pepper

1. To make the tarragon mushrooms, put the oil and butter into a large frying pan over a medium-high heat. Add the mushrooms and cook, stirring, for 10–15 minutes, or until browned. Stir in the garlic and cook for 2 minutes.

2. Pour in the vinegar and as soon as it starts to boil remove the pan from the heat. Transfer the mushrooms to a bowl, add the tarragon and season to taste with salt and pepper. Set aside to cool. Once cooled, cover with clingfilm and set aside.

3. Season the steaks on both sides with the salt and pepper. Heat the oil in a large frying pan over a high heat. Add the steaks and cook for 5–6 minutes on each side for medium-rare, or until cooked to your liking. Cook the steaks in batches if necessary. Set aside to rest for 5 minutes before serving.

4. Add the stock to the hot pan and use a wooden spoon to scrape the sediment from the base of the pan. When the stock has deglazed the pan, add the butter and stir until melted. Add the mushrooms and stir until heated through. Taste and adjust the seasoning if necessary. Serve the steaks with the butter and mushrooms.

Sirloin Steak

with watercress butter

Ingredients

FEEDS 4–6 **PREP 5 mins** **COOK 10 mins**

4 sirloin steaks,
225 g/8 oz each
4 tsp hot sauce
salt and pepper

watercress butter
85 g/3 oz unsalted butter,
softened
4 tbsp chopped
watercress

1. To make the watercress butter, place the butter in a small bowl and mix in the chopped watercress with a fork until combined. Cover with clingfilm and chill for a minimum of 1 hour, or until required.

2. Sprinkle each steak with 1 teaspoon of the hot sauce and season generously with salt and pepper.

3. Heat a griddle pan over a high heat and cook the steaks for 4 minutes on each side for medium-rare, or until cooked to your liking. Cook the steaks in batches if necessary. Set aside to rest for 5 minutes before serving. Serve topped with the watercress butter.

Serve with a classic
steak side dish –
Triple-cooked Chips
(see page 110).

Rump Steak Sandwiches

with mustard dressing

Ingredients

FEEDS 4 **PREP 10 mins** **COOK 25 mins**

8 slices thick white bread
butter, softened, for
spreading
2 handfuls mixed
salad leaves
3 tbsp olive oil
2 onions, thinly sliced
675 g/1 lb 8 oz rump
steak, 2.5 cm/1 inch thick
1 tbsp Worcestershire
sauce
2 tbsp wholegrain
mustard
2 tbsp water
salt and pepper

1. Spread each slice of bread with some butter and add a few salad leaves to the four bottom slices.

2. Heat 2 tablespoons of the oil in a large frying pan over a medium heat. Add the onions and cook, stirring occasionally, for 10–15 minutes, or until softened and golden brown. Using a slotted spoon, transfer to a plate and set aside.

3. Increase the heat to high and add the remaining oil to the pan. Add the steak, season to taste with pepper and seal on both sides. Reduce the heat to medium and cook for 2½–3 minutes on each side for rare, or until cooked to your liking. Transfer the steak to the plate with the onions.

4. Add the Worcestershire sauce, mustard and water to the pan. Use a wooden spoon to scrape the sediment from the base of the pan. When the liquid has deglazed the pan, add the onions and stir. Season to taste with salt and pepper.

5. Thinly slice the steak across the grain, divide between the four bottom slices of bread and cover with the onions and mustard dressing. Cover with the top slices of bread and press down gently. Serve immediately.

Strip Steak

with Béarnaise sauce

Ingredients

FEEDS 4

PREP 15 mins

COOK 30–35 mins

4 strip steaks,
225 g/8 oz each
1 tbsp olive oil
salt and pepper

Béarnaise sauce
1 large bunch tarragon
1 shallot, finely chopped
100 ml/3½ fl oz white
wine vinegar
4 peppercorns
2 egg yolks
200 g/7 oz butter, cubed

1. To make the Béarnaise sauce, remove the most tender leaves of the tarragon, finely chop and set aside. Roughly chop the remaining tarragon and add to a small saucepan with the shallot, vinegar and peppercorns and simmer until it has reduced to about 1 tablespoonful. Strain this through a sieve into a clean heatproof bowl.

2. Bring a separate small saucepan of water to the boil, place the bowl containing the vinegar reduction on top and gently whisk in the egg yolks until the mixture thickens a little. Add the butter a piece at a time and whisk until the sauce is thick. Add the reserved tarragon leaves, stir, and season to taste with salt. Remove from the heat and cover to keep warm while you cook the steaks.

3. Season the steaks with salt and pepper and rub with the oil. Heat a large frying pan over a high heat and add the steaks. Cook for 3–4 minutes on each side for medium-rare, or until cooked to your liking. Set aside to rest for 5 minutes before serving with the sauce.

Porterhouse Steak

with chilli and garlic rub

Ingredients

FEEDS 4 · **PREP 10 mins** · **COOK 10 mins**

4 porterhouse or T-bone
steaks, 350 g/12 oz each

chilli and garlic rub
1 tsp salt
2 tsp pepper
4 tbsp olive oil
3 garlic cloves, crushed
1 tsp chilli flakes

1. Place all of the chilli and garlic rub ingredients in a pestle and mortar and crush to a rough paste. Alternatively, process in a food processor or blender to achieve the desired consistency.

2. Rub the chilli and garlic mixture all over the steaks.

3. Preheat a griddle pan over a medium-high heat and cook the steaks for 5 minutes on each side for medium-rare, or until cooked to your liking. Cook the steaks in batches if necessary. Set aside to rest for 5 minutes before serving.

T-bone Steak

with peppercorn sauce

Ingredients

FEEDS 4 **PREP 10 mins** **COOK 20 mins**

4 T-bone steaks,
350 g/12 oz each
1 tsp salt
1 tsp pepper
2 tbsp olive oil

peppercorn sauce
1 tbsp olive oil
1 tbsp butter
2 shallots, finely chopped
2 garlic cloves, crushed
100 ml/3½ fl oz brandy
200 ml/7 fl oz double cream
1 tbsp Dijon mustard
1 tsp salt
1 tbsp mixed cracked peppercorns

1. To make the peppercorn sauce, heat a saucepan over a medium-low heat, add the oil and butter and then cook the shallots and garlic for 5–10 minutes, or until translucent. Add the brandy and flambé. Add the cream and cook until reduced by half. Then add the mustard, salt and cracked peppercorns. Set aside and keep warm.

2. Season the steaks with the salt and pepper, and rub with olive oil.

3. Preheat a griddle pan over a high heat and cook the steaks for 5 minutes on each side for medium-rare, or until cooked to your liking. Cook the steaks in batches if necessary. Set aside to rest for 5 minutes before serving with the peppercorn sauce.

Steakhouse Burgers

with Gruyère cheese

Ingredients

FEEDS 4 · PREP 20 mins · COOK 10 mins

450 g/1 lb boneless
braising steak (or a
mixture with at least
20 per cent fat)
1 tsp salt
½ tsp pepper
4 burger buns, split
4 slices Gruyère cheese

1. Chop the beef into 2.5-cm/1-inch cubes, then place on a plate, wrap in clingfilm and chill in the refrigerator for 30 minutes.

2. Place half the beef in a food processor or blender. Pulse (do not run the processor) about 15 times. Season the meat with half the salt and half the pepper, and pulse a further 10–15 times until the meat is finely chopped but not over-processed. Remove from the processor and repeat with the remaining beef. Divide into four equal-sized portions and shape each portion into a patty.

3. Heat a griddle pan over a medium-high heat. Add the patties and cook for 3 minutes on each side for medium-rare, or until cooked to your liking. Place a slice of cheese on top of each burger during the last 2 minutes of cooking.

4. Serve immediately, in burger buns with your preferred condiments and sides.

Make the burgers in advance, wrap in greaseproof paper and keep in the refrigerator for 1-2 days.

Flank Steak

in 'the best' barbecue marinade

Ingredients

FEEDS
4–6

PREP
5 mins

COOK
10–15 mins

4 garlic cloves,
finely chopped
4 tbsp olive oil,
plus extra for brushing
55 g/2 oz soft light
brown sugar
2 tbsp red wine vinegar
4 tbsp soy sauce
1 tsp Dijon mustard
1 tsp pepper
800 g/1 lb 12 oz
whole flank steak,
trimmed
salt

1. Put all the ingredients, except the steak and salt, into a large, resealable polythene bag. Seal and shake to combine. Add the steak and reseal the bag, squeezing out most of the air. Chill in the refrigerator for a minimum of 6 hours, or for up to 12 hours if time allows. Remove from the refrigerator 1 hour before cooking, to allow the meat to return to room temperature.

2. Transfer the steak to a large plate, reserving the remaining marinade. Pat the steak dry with kitchen paper and season generously on both sides with salt.

3. Heat a griddle pan over a high heat. Brush a little oil over the surface of the pan and add the steak. Cook for 5–6 minutes on each side for medium-rare, or until cooked to your liking. Set aside to rest for 10 minutes before serving.

4. Meanwhile, pour the marinade into a small saucepan and bring to the boil. Serve the steak sliced across the grain, with the marinade on the side.

Steak Medallions

with beef and beer sauce

Ingredients

1.5 kg/3 lb 5 oz beef fillet
1 tsp salt
1 tsp pepper
2 tbsp olive oil

beef and beer sauce
2 tbsp olive oil
2 tbsp butter
2 shallots, finely chopped
2 garlic cloves, crushed
2 tbsp flour
300 ml/10 fl oz good
quality beer
300 ml/10 fl oz hot
beef stock
2 tbsp Worcestershire
sauce
1 tbsp chopped thyme
1 tbsp chopped parsley
1 tsp salt
1 tsp pepper

1. To make the beef and beer sauce, place a saucepan over a medium heat, add the olive oil and butter and cook the shallots and garlic for 5–10 minutes, or until translucent. Then add the flour and cook for a few minutes, until the flour is beginning to brown. Gradually whisk in the beer, then add the beef stock and Worcestershire sauce. Reduce the sauce until it is the consistency of double cream, then add the thyme, parsley and salt and pepper. Set aside and keep warm.

2. On a chopping board, season the beef fillet with the salt, pepper and olive oil.

3. Preheat a griddle pan over a medium-high heat and cook the beef fillet for 15–20 minutes, ensuring that all sides are sealed. Set aside to rest for 10 minutes before serving, then slice and serve with the beer sauce.

Use a pale ale or American lager, as preferred, to make the sauce.

Beef Wellington

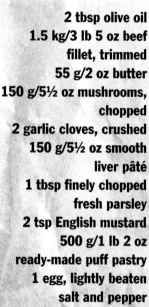

Ingredients

FEEDS
4–6

PREP
30 mins

COOK
1 hour

2 tbsp olive oil
1.5 kg/3 lb 5 oz beef
fillet, trimmed
55 g/2 oz butter
150 g/5½ oz mushrooms,
chopped
2 garlic cloves, crushed
150 g/5½ oz smooth
liver pâté
1 tbsp finely chopped
fresh parsley
2 tsp English mustard
500 g/1 lb 2 oz
ready-made puff pastry
1 egg, lightly beaten
salt and pepper

1. Place a large frying pan over a high heat and add the olive oil. Rub salt and pepper to taste into the beef and seal on all sides for rare. Set aside to cool.

2. Heat the butter in a frying pan over a medium heat, add the mushrooms and fry for 5 minutes. Reduce the heat, add the garlic and fry for another 5 minutes. Put the mushrooms and garlic in a bowl, add the pâté and parsley, and mix together with a fork. Leave to cool.

3. Rub the mustard into the beef fillet. Roll out the pastry into a rectangle large enough to wrap the whole fillet with some to spare. Spread the mushroom paste in the middle of the pastry, leaving a 5-cm/2-inch gap between the paste and the edge of the pastry, and lay the beef on top. Brush the edges of the pastry with beaten egg and fold it over, edges overlapping, and across the meat to completely enclose it.

4. Preheat the oven to 220°C/425°F/Gas Mark 7. Place the wrapped beef in a roasting tin with the pastry join underneath and brush the surface with beaten egg. Place in the refrigerator for 15 minutes to chill, then transfer to the preheated oven and bake for 50 minutes. Check on the pastry after 30 minutes – if it is golden brown, cover with foil to prevent burning. Set aside to rest for 15 minutes before serving.

For well done beef, roast at 220°C/425°F/ Gas Mark 7 for 20 minutes after sealing in the pan.

Rump Steak

with a spicy chilli crust

Ingredients

FEEDS 4–6 **PREP 10 mins** **COOK 20 mins**

2 kg/4 lb 8 oz rump steak

chilli crust
3 tbsp chipotle chilli
paste
1 tsp chilli flakes
3 tbsp light muscovado
sugar
3 tbsp sherry vinegar
4 tbsp olive oil
3 garlic cloves, crushed
2 tsp salt
2 tsp pepper

1. Place all of the crust ingredients in a pestle and mortar and crush to a fine paste. Alternatively, process in a food processor or blender to achieve the desired consistency.

2. Place the steak in a shallow non-metallic dish and cover in the chilli rub, turning a few times to coat. Cover and chill in the refrigerator for a minimum of 4 hours, or for up to 12 hours if time allows.

3. Remove from the refrigerator 2 hours before cooking, to allow the meat to return to room temperature.

4. Preheat a griddle pan over a medium-high heat and cook for 10 minutes on each side for medium-rare, or until cooked to your liking. Set the steak aside to rest for 5 minutes before serving. Slice before serving.

SEVENTY FOUR BEEF CARPACCIO

STEAK TARTARE

Rump Steak in a lemon and thyme marinade

82 SIRLOIN STEAK WITH SESAME AND SPICY ASIAN GREENS

STEAK GOUJONS WITH A CHILLI CRUST AND CUCUMBER DIP

Sirloin Steak in a lime and tequila marinade

SICHUAN STEAK WITH NOODLE AND RADISH SALAD

NINETY STUFFED STEAK WITH GOAT'S CHEESE AND MINT COUSCOUS

SESAME STEAK IN A GINGER MARINADE AND SOY SAUCE BROTH

Tri-tip Steak in an oriental-spiced marinade

FLAT IRON STEAK IN A ROSEMARY AND RED WINE MARINADE

STEAK FOR TWO

Beef Carpaccio

Ingredients

FEEDS 2 **PREP 5 mins**

250 g/9 oz excellent quality beef fillet (cut from the thin end of the fillet)
100 ml/3½ fl oz extra virgin olive oil
25 g/1 oz pine nuts
100 g/3½ oz rocket
10 g/¼ oz Parmesan cheese
1 tsp truffle oil (optional)
salt and pepper

1. Put the beef in the freezer for 1 hour before use, to firm it up before slicing. Trim any fat or sinew from the beef, then cut the fillet into slices as thinly as possible.

2. Lay a slice of beef on a chopping board and, using a flat, broad knife, press against the meat, pushing down hard and pulling across the beef in a spreading motion. Repeat with all the beef slices.

3. Pour a little pool of olive oil into a wide dish. Place a layer of beef on the oil, season lightly with salt and pepper and pour over some more olive oil. Repeat until all the beef has been seasoned in this way. Chill in the refrigerator for at least 30 minutes, or for up to 2 hours if time allows. Meanwhile, toast the pine nuts in a dry frying pan over a medium heat, until lightly browned, and set aside.

4. Pile a bed of rocket onto the serving plates, remove the beef slices from the marinade and divide evenly between the plates. Scatter with the pine nuts and shave the Parmesan cheese over, using a vegetable peeler. Drizzle over a few drops of truffle oil, if using, and serve.

Steak Tartare

Ingredients

250 g/9 oz excellent
quality beef fillet or
sirloin steak
1 tbsp finely chopped
parsley
1 tbsp finely chopped
capers
1 tbsp finely chopped
shallots
1 tbsp finely chopped
gherkins
2 dashes hot sauce
2 dashes Worcestershire
sauce
1 tbsp Dijon mustard
½ tsp salt
2 egg yolks
(kept separate)

FEEDS
2

PREP
15 mins

1. Chill all the ingredients, a chopping board and mixing bowl for 20 minutes before you begin. Then remove from the refrigerator and finely chop the steak until minced.

2. Place the minced steak in the chilled bowl. Add all the remaining ingredients, except the egg yolks, and mix them into the beef with a fork.

3. Shape the mixture into two round patties and make an indent in the middle of each. Place in the refrigerator until ready to serve. To serve, place each patty in the middle of a plate and lay an egg yolk in the indent.

Serve with a lightly
poached egg (still
runny in the middle),
if preferred

Rump Steak

in a lemon and thyme marinade

Ingredients

FEEDS 2   **PREP 10 mins**   **COOK 10 mins**

2 rump steaks,
280 g/10 oz each
2 tbsp extra virgin
olive oil
juice and zest of 1 lemon
1 small bunch thyme,
leaves picked

marinade
4 tbsp olive oil
1 small bunch thyme,
leaves picked
2 garlic cloves, crushed
juice and zest of 1 lemon
1 tsp salt
1 tsp pepper

1. Place all of the marinade ingredients into a shallow non-metallic dish, large enough to hold both of the steaks in a single layer. Mix the ingredients together.

2. Add the steaks to the marinade, turning a few times to coat. Cover and chill in the refrigerator for a minimum of 4 hours, or for up to 12 hours if time allows. Turn once, mid-way through marinating. Remove from the refrigerator 1 hour before cooking, to allow the meat to return to room temperature.

3. Preheat a griddle pan over a high heat and cook the steaks for 5 minutes on each side for medium-rare, or until cooked to your liking. Set aside to rest for 5 minutes before serving.

4. Once rested, slice the steaks and serve drizzled with the olive oil and lemon juice, and sprinkled with the lemon zest and thyme leaves.

Sirloin Steak

with sesame and spicy Asian greens

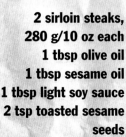

Ingredients

FEEDS 2 **PREP 15 mins** **COOK 15 mins**

2 sirloin steaks,
280 g/10 oz each
1 tbsp olive oil
1 tbsp sesame oil
1 tbsp light soy sauce
2 tsp toasted sesame
seeds
1 tsp pepper

spicy oriental greens
1 tbsp olive oil
2 garlic cloves,
finely chopped
2-cm/¾-inch piece
ginger, finely chopped
1 small red chilli, finely
chopped
2 spring onions,
finely sliced
400 g/14 oz trimmed
Asian greens (such as
kai-lan and pak choi)
2 tbsp light soy sauce
1 tbsp sesame seeds

1. Season the steaks with olive oil, sesame oil, soy sauce, sesame seeds and pepper.

2. Preheat a large frying pan over a medium-high heat and cook the steaks for 5 minutes on each side for medium-rare, or until cooked to your liking. Set aside to rest for 5 minutes before serving.

3. Meanwhile, return the frying pan to the heat and add the olive oil, garlic, ginger, chilli, spring onions and greens and stir-fry until the greens begin to wilt. Add the soy sauce and sesame seeds, and serve immediately with the steak.

Steak Goujons

with a chilli crust and cucumber dip

FEEDS 2   **PREP** 20 mins   **COOK** 15 mins

Ingredients

vegetable oil, for
deep-frying

steak goujons
2 tbsp flour
2 eggs, beaten
150 g/5½ oz panko
breadcrumbs
1 tsp chilli flakes
1 tsp smoked paprika
1 tsp salt
1 tsp pepper
300 g/10½ oz beef fillet,
cut into strips

cucumber dip
200 ml/7 fl oz natural
yogurt
½ cucumber, grated
small bunch mint,
chopped
juice and zest of 1 lemon
1 shallot, finely chopped
salt and pepper
pinch of smoked
paprika, to garnish

1. To make the steak goujons, place the flour, eggs and breadcrumbs into three separate shallow dishes. Season the breadcrumbs with the chilli flakes, paprika, salt and pepper. Dust each steak strip in the flour, then dip in the eggs and then coat in breadcrumbs and set aside.

2. Heat enough oil for deep-frying in a large saucepan or deep-fat fryer to 180–190°C/350–375°F, or until a cube of bread browns in 30 seconds.

3. Meanwhile, to make the cucumber dip, mix together all of the ingredients, apart from the paprika, in a small bowl. Chill in the refrigerator until required.

4. Cook the beef goujons in the oil in batches, for 8–10 minutes or until golden brown, then drain on kitchen paper and serve with the cucumber dip sprinkled with the paprika.

Sirloin Steak

in a lime and tequila marinade

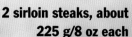
Ingredients

 FEEDS 2 PREP 10 mins COOK 10 mins

2 sirloin steaks, about
225 g/8 oz each

marinade
1 tbsp olive oil
1½ tbsp tequila
1½ tbsp freshly squeezed
orange juice
½ tbsp freshly squeezed
lime juice
2 garlic cloves, crushed
1 tsp chilli powder
1 tsp ground cumin
½ tsp dried oregano
salt and pepper

1. Place all of the marinade ingredients into a shallow non-metallic dish, large enough to hold both of the steaks in a single layer. Mix the ingredients together.

2. Add the steaks to the marinade, turning a few times to coat. Cover, and chill in the refrigerator for a minimum of 2 hours, or for up to 12 hours if time allows. Turn once, mid-way through marinating.

3. Remove from the refrigerator 1 hour before cooking, to allow the meat to return to room temperature. Reserve the remaining marinade.

4. Preheat a griddle pan over a high heat and cook the steaks for 3–4 minutes on each side for medium-rare, or until cooked to your liking. Baste frequently with the remaining marinade. Set the steak aside to rest for 5 minutes before serving.

This marinade mixture is perfect for making a quick corn relish – make a second batch and stir in sweetcorn, chopped red pepper and fresh coriander.

Sichuan Steak

with noodle and radish salad

Ingredients

FEEDS 2

PREP 5 mins

COOK 10 mins

175 g/6 oz sirloin steak
40 g/1½ oz egg noodles
½ small red onion,
thinly sliced
3 radishes, sliced
2 handfuls of tatsoi,
mustard greens and
rocket
1 tbsp groundnut oil
½ tsp Sichuan pepper

marinade
2 tsp Chinese rice wine
¼ tbsp soy sauce
2 tsp sugar
1 tbsp hoisin sauce
1.5-cm/½-inch piece
fresh ginger, grated

dressing
1 tsp Sichuan pepper
1 tbsp light soy sauce
1 tbsp rice vinegar
1 tbsp sesame oil

1. Place all of the marinade ingredients into a shallow non-metallic dish, large enough to hold the steak in a single layer. Mix the ingredients together.

2. Trim any fat from the steak. Slice into thin strips and add to the marinade, turning a few times to coat. Cover, and chill in the refrigerator for 30 minutes. Remove from the refrigerator 30 minutes before cooking, to allow the meat to return to room temperature.

3. Cook the noodles in a saucepan of boiling water for 3–4 minutes, or cook according to the packet instructions, until tender. Drain and allow to cool. Snip into shorter lengths using kitchen scissors and set aside.

4. Place all of the dressing ingredients into a small bowl and whisk until well blended. Combine the noodles, onion, radishes and salad leaves in a large bowl. Pour two thirds of the dressing over the salad. Toss to distribute the noodles, then divide between individual serving plates.

5. Heat a wok over a medium-high heat, then add the groundnut oil and the Sichuan pepper. Stir for a few seconds to flavour the oil. Add the steak and marinade, and stir-fry for 4–5 minutes until caramelized. Remove with a slotted spoon, and scatter over the salad. Pour over the remaining dressing and serve immediately.

Sichuan pepper has a numbing effect on the tongue and creates a slight tingling sensation.

Stuffed Steak

with goat's cheese and mint couscous

Ingredients

FEEDS 2 PREP 20 mins COOK 15 mins

2 sirloin steaks,
280 g/10 oz each
1 tbsp olive oil
salt and pepper

goat's cheese stuffing
1 garlic clove, crushed
100 g/3½ oz soft goat's
cheese, chopped
100 g/3½ oz cherry
tomatoes, chopped
2 tbsp chopped
flat-leaf parsley,
1 tbsp olive oil
½ tsp pepper
½ tsp salt

mint couscous
100 g/3½ oz couscous
1 tbsp extra virgin
olive oil
small bunch flat-leaf
parsley, chopped
small bunch mint,
chopped
juice and zest of 1 lemon
1 shallot, finely chopped
1 large tomato, chopped

1. To make the goat's cheese stuffing, place all of the ingredients into a small non-metallic bowl and mix well. Set aside.

2. On a chopping board, season the steaks generously with salt and pepper and rub with olive oil. With a sharp knife cut a slit in the non-fatty side of the steaks, to create a pocket (do not cut through the whole steak). Fill the pockets with the stuffing mixture and set aside.

3. To make the couscous, place the couscous and olive oil in a small heatproof bowl, and cover with boiling water. Cover the bowl with clingfilm and leave for 2 minutes. Remove the clingfilm and break up the grains with a fork until light and fluffy. Add the remaining ingredients, season to taste with salt and pepper, mix well and set aside.

4. Preheat a griddle pan over a medium-high heat and cook the steaks for 5 minutes on each side for medium, or until cooked to your liking. Set the steaks aside to rest for 5 minutes before serving with the couscous.

Sesame Steak

in a ginger marinade and soy sauce broth

Ingredients

225 g/8 oz sirloin steak
groundnut oil,
for deep-frying
¼ tsp toasted sesame oil
½ tsp chilli oil (optional)
1 tsp sesame seeds,
to garnish

marinade
1.5-cm/½-inch piece
fresh ginger, thinly sliced
1 spring onion, cut into
2–3 pieces
1 tsp rice wine
1 tsp toasted sesame oil

soy sauce broth
125 ml/4 fl oz beef stock
½ tsp soy sauce
½ tsp rice wine or dry
sherry
pinch of salt
1 tsp sugar
½ tsp fennel seeds,
crushed
1.5-cm/½-inch piece
cinnamon stick

1. Slice the steak into thin strips and flatten with a meat mallet.

2. Place all of the marinade ingredients into a shallow non-metallic dish, large enough to hold all of the steak strips in a single layer. Mix the ingredients together. Add the steak to the marinade, turning a few times to coat. Cover, and chill in the refrigerator for 30 minutes. Remove from the refrigerator 1 hour before cooking, to allow the meat to return to room temperature. Remove and discard the ginger and spring onion.

3. Heat enough groundnut oil for deep-frying in a large wok to 180–190°C/350–375°F, or until a cube of bread browns in 30 seconds. Add the steak strips to the wok and fry for 1 minute, stirring occasionally. Remove with a slotted spoon and drain on kitchen paper.

4. Return the oil temperature to 180°C/350°F. Return the meat to the wok and fry for a further 2–3 minutes, until the strips are crisp and dark brown. Remove and drain again.

5. To make the broth, bring the stock to the boil in a separate saucepan. Add the remaining ingredients and simmer for 1 minute, then add the steak strips. Simmer over a gentle heat for 15–20 minutes, stirring from time to time, until the liquid has evaporated and the meat is sticky. Remove the cinnamon stick.

6. Stir in the sesame oil, and the chilli oil, if using. Sprinkle with the sesame seeds and serve warm.

Appetizingly chewy, these beef slivers make a great snack or nibble to serve with drinks.

Tri-tip Steak

in an oriental-spiced marinade

Ingredients

2 tri-tip or bottom sirloin
steaks, 280 g/10 oz each

marinade
1 tbsp olive oil
1 tbsp sesame oil
1 tsp white sugar
1 tbsp Chinese black
vinegar
2-cm/¾-inch piece fresh
ginger, peeled and finely
chopped
1 garlic clove, crushed
1 tbsp toasted sesame
seeds
1 tbsp light soy sauce
1 tsp pepper

1. Place all of the marinade ingredients into a shallow non-metallic dish, large enough to hold both of the steaks in a single layer. Mix the ingredients together.

2. Add the steaks to the marinade, turning a few times to coat. Cover and chill in the refrigerator for a minimum of 4 hours, or for up to 12 hours if time allows. Turn once, mid-way through marinating. Remove from the refrigerator 1 hour before cooking, to allow the meat to return to room temperature. Discard the marinade.

3. Preheat a griddle pan over a high heat and cook the steaks for 5 minutes on each side for medium-rare, or until cooked to your liking. Set the steaks aside to rest for 5 minutes before serving.

Flat Iron Steak

in a rosemary and red wine marinade

Ingredients

FEEDS 2 **PREP 10 mins** **COOK 10 mins**

2 flat iron steaks,
280 g/10 oz each
1 tbsp olive oil
1 tbsp butter

marinade
2 tbsp extra virgin
olive oil
200 ml/7 fl oz good
quality red wine
1 small bunch thyme,
leaves picked
1 small bunch rosemary,
leaves picked
2 garlic cloves, crushed
1 tsp salt
1 tsp pepper

1. Place all of the marinade ingredients into a shallow non-metallic dish, large enough to hold both of the steaks in a single layer. Mix the ingredients together.

2. Add the steaks to the marinade, turning a few times to coat. Cover and chill in the refrigerator for a minimum of 4 hours, or for up to 12 hours if time allows. Turn once, mid-way through marinating.

3. Remove from the refrigerator 1 hour before cooking to allow the meat to return to room temperature. Reserve the remaining marinade.

4. Preheat a large frying pan over a medium-high heat and add the oil and butter. Cook the steaks for 5 minutes on each side for medium-rare, or until cooked to your liking. Set the steak aside to rest for 5 minutes before serving.

5. Meanwhile, add the remaining marinade to the frying pan and cook until reduced by half. Serve the steaks with the red wine marinade poured over the top.

HASH BROWNS

ONE HUNDRED

MACARONI AND CHEESE

104 Creamed Spinach

106 HOME-MADE MUSTARD 107 MAYONNAISE

OOOOO ONION RINGS

TRIPLE-COOKED CHIPS
TRIPLE-COOKED CHIPS
TRIPLE-COOKED CHIPS **110**

CORN ON THE COB WITH BLUE CHEESE DIP

TOMATO KETCHUP 114 BARBECUE SAUCE 115

116 *Scalloped Potatoes*

CAULIFLOWER BAKE

122 Coleslaw NEW POTATOES WITH GARLIC AND CHILLI BUTTER

CHAPTER
FOUR
SAUCES AND SIDES

Hash Browns

FEEDS 4   **PREP 10 mins**   **COOK 40 mins**

Ingredients

1 kg/2 lb 4 oz maris piper
potatoes
2 tbsp olive oil
1 large onion, sliced
1 egg, beaten
150 g/5½ oz instant
potato powder
vegetable oil, for
deep-frying
salt and pepper

1. Place the potatoes in a large saucepan of lukewarm, salted water. Bring the water to the boil, and when the water reaches boiling point, remove the pan from the heat and leave to cool.

2. In a separate frying pan, heat the olive oil over a low heat. Add the onions and fry for 5–7 minutes, until soft and translucent, but not browned.

3. Once the potatoes are cool enough to handle, coarsely grate them into a large bowl. Add the fried onions, egg and potato powder. Mix well and season to taste with salt and pepper.

4. Heat enough oil for deep-frying in a large saucepan or deep-fryer to 180–190°C/350–375°F, or until a cube of bread browns in 30 seconds.

5. Meanwhile, roll the potato mixture into walnut sized balls and flatten each into a patty shape. Fry in batches in the preheated oil until golden and leave to drain on kitchen paper before serving.

Macaroni and Cheese

Ingredients

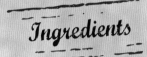 

FEEDS 4   **PREP 10 mins**   **COOK 30 mins**

250 g/9 oz dried macaroni pasta
600 ml/1 pint milk
½ tsp grated nutmeg
55 g/2 oz butter
55 g/2 oz plain flour
200 g/7 oz Cheddar cheese, grated
55 g/2 oz Parmesan cheese, grated
salt and pepper

1. Bring a large saucepan of lightly salted water to the boil. Add the pasta and cook for 8–10 minutes, or until tender but still firm to the bite. Remove from the heat, drain and set aside.

2. Put the milk and nutmeg into a saucepan over a low heat and heat until warm, but do not bring to the boil.

3. Melt the butter in a heavy-based saucepan over a low heat, then add the flour and stir to make a roux. Cook gently for 2 minutes. Add the hot milk a little at a time, whisking it into the roux, then cook for about 10–15 minutes to make a loose sauce.

4. Add three quarters of the Cheddar cheese and all the Parmesan cheese and stir through until they have melted. Season to taste with salt and pepper and remove from the heat.

5. Preheat the grill to high. Put the macaroni into a shallow heatproof dish, then pour the sauce over. Scatter the remaining cheese over the top and place the dish under the preheated grill. Grill until the cheese begins to brown.

For a crisp topping, sprinkle 25 g/1 oz of fresh breadcrumbs over the top, along with the Cheddar.

Creamed Spinach

Ingredients

15 g/½ oz butter
900 g/2 lb young spinach leaves
4 tbsp single cream
½ tsp freshly grated nutmeg
salt and pepper

1. Melt the butter in a large frying pan, add the spinach and cook, stirring, until the leaves are wilted.

2. Continue to cook over a medium heat, stirring occasionally, until most of the liquid has evaporated.

3. Stir in the cream and nutmeg, and season to taste with salt and pepper. Serve immediately.

Swap the single cream for Greek yogurt, for a healthier version of this classic side dish.

Home-made Mustard

Ingredients

MAKES
175 ml/6 fl oz

PREP
15 mins

3 tbsp brown mustard
seeds
3 tbsp cider vinegar
1–2 tbsp water
3 tbsp mustard powder
2 tsp salt
2 tsp honey

1. Put the mustard seeds into a small non-metallic container with the vinegar and enough water to cover completely. Set aside for two days, covered, at room temperature.

2. Strain the mustard seeds, reserving the liquid. Place the mustard seeds into a pestle and mortar and crush to a rough paste – the finer the paste, the spicier the mustard will be.

3. Place the crushed mustard seeds into a small bowl with the mustard powder, salt and honey. Add the reserved vinegar water and stir.

4. Place in a sterilized jar, seal and refrigerate for at least 2 days before serving. Once opened, store in the refrigerator and consume within 2 weeks.

Mayonnaise

Ingredients

MAKES
300 ml/10 fl oz

PREP
15 mins

2 large egg yolks
2 tsp Dijon mustard
¾ tsp salt, or to taste
2–3 tbsp lemon juice
300 ml/10 fl oz
sunflower oil
white pepper

1. Mix the egg yolks with the Dijon mustard, salt and white pepper to taste in a food processor orblender. Add 2 tablespoons lemon juice and process again.

2. With the processor still running, add the oil, drop by drop at first. When the sauce begins to thicken, the oil can be added in a slow, steady stream. If the mayonnaise becomes too thick, add another 1 tablespoon of lemon juice.

3. Place in a sterilized jar, seal and refrigerate. Use at once. Once opened, store in the refrigerator and consume within 3 days.

Onion Rings

Ingredients

FEEDS 4

PREP 15 mins

COOK 15 mins

115 g/4 oz plain flour
pinch of salt
1 egg
150 ml/5 fl oz
semi-skimmed milk
4 large onions
vegetable oil, for
deep-frying
salt and pepper

1. To make the batter, sift the flour and salt into a large bowl and make a well in the centre. Break the egg into the well and gently beat with a whisk. Gradually whisk in the milk, drawing the flour from the sides of the bowl into the liquid in the centre to form a smooth batter.

2. Leaving the onions whole, slice widthways into 5-mm/¼-inch slices, then separate each slice into rings.

3. Heat the oil in a deep-fat fryer or deep, heavy-based saucepan to 180–190°C/350–375°F, or until a cube of bread browns in 30 seconds.

4. Using the tines of a fork, pick up several onions rings at a time and dip in the batter. Let any excess batter drip off, then add the onions to the oil and deep-fry for 1–2 minutes until they rise to the surface of the oil and become crisp and golden brown. Remove from the oil, drain on kitchen paper and keep warm while deep-frying the remaining onion rings in batches.

5. Season the onion rings with salt and pepper to taste, then serve immediately.

Triple-cooked Chips

Ingredients

FEEDS
4

PREP
10 mins

COOK
15 mins

900 g/2 lb potatoes
1 litre/1¾ pints
vegetable oil
sea salt

1. Cut the potatoes into 5 x 5-mm/¼ x ¼-inch sticks. Soak the cut potatoes in a bowl of cold water for 5 minutes, then drain and rinse.

2. Bring a medium-sized saucepan of lightly salted water to the boil over a high heat. Add the potatoes, bring back to the boil and cook for 3–4 minutes, until the potatoes begin to soften. Drain the potatoes and spread on a baking sheet lined with kitchen paper. Refrigerate for a minimum of 1 hour or for up to 12 hours if time allows.

3. Place the oil in a large heavy-based saucepan or a deep-fat fryer. If using a saucepan, attach a deep-frying thermometer. Heat the oil to 180–190°C/350–375°F, or until a cube of bread browns in 30 seconds. Carefully add the cut potatoes, in batches, if necessary, to avoid overcrowding. Cook for 3–4 minutes, until beginning to brown. Remove using tongs and drain on a plate lined with kitchen paper.

4. Return the oil to 180–190°C/350–375°F, then add the potatoes again and fry for 3–5 minutes, until golden brown and crisp. Remove from the oil and drain on a plate lined with kitchen paper. Season generously with sea salt and serve immediately.

Corn on the Cob

with blue cheese dip

Ingredients

140 g/5 oz Danish Blue
cheese
140 g/5 oz curd cheese
125 ml/4 fl oz natural
Greek yogurt
6 corn cobs, in their
husks
salt and pepper

1. Crumble the Danish Blue cheese, then place in a bowl. Beat with a wooden spoon until creamy. Beat in the curd cheese until thoroughly blended. Gradually beat in the yogurt and season to taste with salt and pepper. Cover with clingfilm and leave to chill in the refrigerator until required. Meanwhile, preheat the oven to 220°C/425°F/Gas Mark 7.

2. Fold back the husks on each corn cob and remove the silks. Smooth the husks back into place. Cut out six rectangles of foil, each large enough to enclose a corn cob. Wrap the corn cobs in the foil.

3. Place the corn cobs in the preheated oven and cook for 20 minutes. Unwrap the corn cobs and discard the foil. Peel back the husk on one side of each and trim off with a sharp knife. Serve with the blue cheese dressing.

Tomato Ketchup

Ingredients

2 tbsp olive oil
1 red onion, peeled and chopped
2 garlic cloves, chopped
250 g/9 oz plum tomatoes, chopped
250 g/9 oz canned chopped tomatoes
½ tsp ground ginger
½ tsp chilli powder
40 g/1½ oz dark brown sugar
100 ml/3½ fl oz red wine vinegar
salt and pepper

MAKES 250 ml/9 fl oz   **PREP** 10 mins   **COOK** 20 mins

1. Heat the olive oil in a large saucepan and add the onion, garlic and tomatoes. Add the ginger and chilli and season with salt and pepper to taste. Cook for 15 minutes, or until soft.

2. Pour the mixture into a food processor or blender and blend well. Sieve thoroughly to remove all the seeds. Return the mixture to the pan and add the sugar and vinegar. Return to the boil and cook until it is the consistency of shop-bought ketchup.

3. Transfer to sterilized jars, leave to cool completely, then seal. Store in a cool dark place and refrigerate once opened.

Barbecue Sauce

MAKES
255 ml/9 fl oz

PREP
15 mins

COOK
20 mins

Ingredients

1 tbsp olive oil
1 small onion, finely chopped
2–3 garlic cloves, crushed
1 fresh red jalapeño chilli, deseeded and finely chopped (optional)
2 tsp tomato purée
1 tsp dry mustard, or to taste
1 tbsp red wine vinegar
1 tbsp Worcestershire sauce
2–3 tsp muscovado sugar
300 ml/10 fl oz water

1. Heat the oil in a small heavy-based saucepan, add the onion, garlic and chilli, if using, and gently sauté, stirring frequently, for 3 minutes, or until beginning to soften. Remove from the heat.

2. Blend the tomato purée with the mustard, vinegar and Worcestershire sauce to a paste, then stir into the onion mixture with 2 teaspoons of the sugar. Mix well, then gradually stir in the water.

3. Return to the heat and bring to the boil, stirring frequently. Reduce the heat and gently simmer, stirring occasionally, for 15 minutes. Taste and add the remaining sugar, if liked. Serve hot or cold.

Scalloped Potatoes

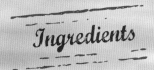

Ingredients

FEEDS 4

PREP 10 mins

COOK 1½ hours

4 large jacket potatoes, about 400 g/14 oz each
oil, for brushing
2 tbsp milk or single cream
2 eggs, separated
100 g/3½ oz Cheddar cheese, grated
15 g/½ oz butter
4 spring onions, finely chopped
salt and pepper

1. Preheat the oven to 200°C/400°F/Gas Mark 6. Place the potatoes on a baking sheet, brush with oil and rub with salt. Bake in the preheated oven for 1–1¼ hours until tender.

2. Cut a slice from the top of the potatoes and scoop out the flesh, leaving about a 5-mm/¼-inch thick shell. Put the flesh into a bowl. Add the milk, egg yolks and half the cheese and mash together.

3. Melt the butter in a small saucepan, add the spring onions and stir-fry for 1–2 minutes until soft. Stir into the potato mixture and season to taste with salt and pepper.

4. Whisk the egg whites in a grease-free bowl until they hold soft peaks. Fold them lightly into the potato mixture, then spoon the mixture back into the shells.

5. Place the filled potatoes on the baking sheet and sprinkle the remaining cheese on top. Bake for 15–20 minutes until golden. Serve immediately.

Cauliflower Bake

 **Ingredients**

 FEEDS 4–6

 PREP 10 mins

 COOK 30 mins

600 g/1 lb 5 oz cauliflower florets (1 medium cauliflower)

150 ml/5 fl oz dry white wine

1 bay leaf

450 ml/16 fl oz milk

25 g/1 oz butter, cut into pieces

25 g/1 oz plain flour

70 g/2½ oz mature Cheddar cheese, grated

40 g/1½ oz Parmesan cheese, grated

1 tsp English mustard

1 tbsp snipped fresh chives

1 tbsp chopped fresh parsley

salt

1. Cook the cauliflower in a large saucepan of lightly salted boiling water for 6–8 minutes until tender but still firm to the bite. Drain and set aside. Preheat the oven to 200°C/400°F/Gas Mark 6.

2. Place the wine and bay leaf in a saucepan. Boil rapidly until the wine is reduced by half. Add the milk, butter and flour and whisk with a hand whisk until the butter has melted. Continue whisking until the sauce boils and thickens. Simmer for 1 minute.

3. Remove from the heat. Mix the cheeses together and stir two thirds into the sauce until smooth, then stir in the mustard, chives and parsley. Remove and discard the bay leaf.

4. Spoon a little of the sauce over the base of a shallow baking dish. Tip the cauliflower into the dish and spread out in an even layer. Spoon the remaining sauce over the top and sprinkle with the remaining cheese. Bake in the preheated oven for 20 minutes until lightly browned and bubbling. Serve immediately.

Wine, fresh herbs and punchy Parmesan have been added to this modern version of the classic dish.

Coleslaw

Ingredients

150 ml/5 fl oz mayonnaise
(see page 107)
150 ml/5 fl oz natural
yogurt
dash of hot sauce
1 head of white cabbage
4 carrots
1 green pepper
salt and pepper

1. To make the dressing, mix the mayonnaise, yogurt, hot sauce and salt and pepper to taste together in a small bowl. Chill in the refrigerator until required.

2. Cut the cabbage in half and then into quarters. Remove and discard the tough centre stalk. Finely shred the cabbage leaves. Wash the leaves under cold running water and dry thoroughly on kitchen paper. Peel the carrots and roughly grate or shred in a food processor or on a mandoline. Quarter and deseed the pepper and cut the flesh into thin strips.

3. Mix the vegetables together in a large serving bowl and toss to mix. Pour over the dressing and toss until the vegetables are well coated. Cover and chill in the refrigerator until required.

Reduce the white cabbage to ½ head, and add ½ head of red cabbage for a more colourful slaw.

New Potatoes

with garlic and chilli butter

FEEDS 4

PREP 10 mins

COOK 20 mins

Ingredients

700 g/1 lb 9 oz baby new potatoes
40 g/1½ oz butter
1 garlic clove, finely chopped
1 red chilli, deseeded and finely chopped
salt and pepper
chopped fresh coriander leaves, to garnish

1. Bring a large saucepan of lightly salted water to the boil, add the potatoes, bring back to the boil and cook for 15 minutes, or until tender. Drain and set aside.

2. Melt the butter in a large saucepan, add the garlic and chilli and gently fry for 30 seconds, without browning.

3. Add the potatoes and stir to coat in the butter, then season to taste with salt and pepper. Sprinkle with the coriander and serve hot.

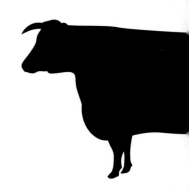